Signs of Life

Poems for remembering

MEG BLOOM

First published by Bloom House Press 2019

Copyright © 2019 Meg Bloom

All rights reserved.

ISBN: 978-0-6486505-0-8

For my family: past, present and future.

CONTENTS

1. Prologue — 3
2. Trauma — 9
3. Grief — 31
4. Loss — 51
5. Love — 67
6. Learning — 85
7. Hope — 105

PROLOGUE

Signs of Life
is a collection of poems
about the feelings
and experiences
that make us alive:

trauma
grief
loss
love
learning
hope

it offers moments
to reflect
on both the pain
and joy
that fill our lives
and what
we can learn from them

TRAUMA

SIGNS OF LIFE

silk red
is the river between us
a dark pool
brimming with crimson splendour
atop the ash and dust

life wilts softly
kindly
just moments after
the violence ensued
in the pale light of the morning

your sudden absence
an unfamiliar void
I cannot fill

your white, soul-less gaze
cold and inescapable

where does life
and death begin
along this river of culpability
where love turns to pain
in its merciless end

— *silk river*

please don't cry
too much
I haven't cleaned the gutters
and I don't want
to cause a flood

— *repression*

SIGNS OF LIFE

I'm afraid
of opening the box
the ribbons
are deceptively colourful
but I know
the darkness inside
is endless
and will crush me
ruthlessly
under its power

— *pandora*

sometimes I lose the present
like a lace curtain
has fallen
between me and the world

I am neither here
nor gone
but somewhere in between
where the damp air fuels the rot

extracted
through a cold vacuum
from the last
vestiges of my body

like a lost ship
drifting in exile
calling out to life
in the distance

– *dissociation*

SIGNS OF LIFE

words
are the hardest
to say
time has stolen
and frozen them
in my throat
like cement
hardening
in a mine shaft

– frozen

find me
in the space between
the light
and the dark
in the crevices
where lonely hearts hibernate
to survive

this taut body
a soft cloak of armour
to repel all wondering eyes and
wondering hands
that follow me through
the days
and the nightmares

self-destructive
preservation
the only thing more bearable
than the truth
spoken from the crib:
that which is unspeakable
in this life

— *the body keeper*

SIGNS OF LIFE

the truth is, I love to lose
the pain is familiar
like cutting myself
when no one is watching

– *counting losses*

tell me
how you feel
let me comfort you
carry you
tell you everything
will be ok
lean on me
when the world
is too much
when the stress
and the pain
cripples you
depend on me
to lift you out of bed
to dress you
nourish you
push you
trust me
to always be there
to keep you
from falling apart
expect me
need me
use me
then watch me break
underneath you

— *burdens*

SIGNS OF LIFE

I wish I could get angry
like you
so unfiltered
and alive

it must be good
to feel things
in your own body

— *filtered*

I think I heard you say
that was nice
though I'm not sure who you were trying to convince.
maybe what you meant was
sorry
I thought you were just here for me to do what I want with
or
excuse me, I hope you don't mind if I just rip you open
stuff myself inside you and sew you back together again
with
that was nice
as you glanced back
with a pang of guilt
swiftly buried for the sake of your own
conscience –
I'm sure
that was nice.
In fact I wish I felt as guilty
because resentment at my own
paralysis
stings
burns
from the place you invaded me
to the back of my throat
where I have to carry you around
inside of me
long after you picked up
your clothes
and left.

– *nice boys*

SIGNS OF LIFE

I can still feel you
inside of me
I never wanted you there

— *scar*

I see you
looming
in the crevices
stroking the follicles
on the back of my neck
with your breath

an absent face
in an ethereal dream
picks me apart
piece by piece
and defeat
grips me

the exits have faded
and we are alone
eclipsed by your shadow
I drown
in your hunger
tonight, I will let you take me

— *depression*

don't look at me like that
so shrill
and discerning
you're not allowed to see
what I hide
in the cupboard

— *secrets*

your bones
are just
a frail cocoon

for
a slowing heart
losing rhythm

calling out for
my
touch

but
brittle
between my fingertips

unsung secrets
drip
drip
from your lips

— *bones*

eating is overrated
she said

no matter how much
or little
I feed my body
it is still ugly

so I might as well stop
altogether

and yet
only love can feed beauty

— *hunger*

I'm so tired
of being your sponge
soaking up
all the feelings
you spill out onto the table

— *sponge*

SIGNS OF LIFE

no matter how much
you reject me
in the end
I'm always there for you

what would I know?
I'm just
someone with an opinion

— *contempt*

I must be your mirror
you hate everything about yourself
and you see it
in me

— *conflict*

GRIEF

all the storms you could not weather
you were like my umbrella
protective, feeble
turned inside out and folded back
but never the same

all the pain you could not carry
it festered inside you
until you succumbed to its shadow
caustic, like poison
corroding you from within

all the burdens you could not share
you whispered them to the sky
in sweet relief
but they followed you to the heavens
relentless and unforgiving

all the beauty you left behind
now sings to you in your sleep
watches your children grow
and promises to keep them safe
until the next life

— *storms*

I lost you
somewhere along the way
in a flicker of time
so fast
when you decided, beyond dissuasion
that you were not meant for this world

how could I reach you
when you were already gone
but standing
right in front of me?

— *unreachable*

your children ask me
where you have gone
I say
I don't know
but that you will visit them
in their dreams

not sure
if that fits in with your plans

– for your children

hello
what is it like
up there?
it's hard to say I miss you
I'm not sure
that I do
but
slow steps, I guess.

I thought of you again today
for the first time
there wasn't pain
just
coldness.
some might say that's progress,
but it hurt all the same.

do you think of me
sometimes
and all that could have been?
what we could have
made
with these hearts
and these four hands?

…

maybe.
maybe not.
but in case you ever wonder
just know that I would have
tried.
tried to love you
just as much as they do
up there.

— *night whispers*

where did you go?
it feels
like you are stuck in my chest
pulling me down
so tight
every inch of me
burns in your absence
I need you
to come back

— *breathless*

they say, at least
you're no longer in pain
but what of the pain
you passed on to me?

they think, now
you will rest in peace
but what good is peace
knowing you chose to leave?

perhaps peace
is learning to accept
that you're gone
despite all the pain that brings.

– *navigating peace*

I'm sorry
I didn't see
or listen
or recognise
the pain you were feeling
I regret it
every day

– *guilt*

you are there
across the plains
beneath the sky
within the sea
always swimming
far away
from the capture
of my embrace
I know
that you need it
but you are too
self-destructive
to succumb
to its peace

— *saviour*

pain
is a spectrum
from the prick of a finger
to a broken bone
and a broken heart
one side stings
the middle
steals your breath
and the other end burns
slowly
so numb
you feel nothing at all
and nothing else ever hurts
quite as much

— pain

you branded me
with hot, searing hands
burnt deep
to stay forever
where I can trace your mark
in circles
through the dark.
is this what you meant
when you said you
would never leave me?

— branded

where is this elusive sleep
that hides from me each night
teasing me
with lucid dreaming
and wakefulness
guiding me gently into darkness
to then desert me
with such cruelty?

— *insomnia*

silence befalls the angels at night
as the frost bites
at children's toes in
the dampness

there are no guardians here
at the bottom of the world
where the wretched
wait for death
in all its kindness

what fool
dreams of salvation
when even the angels
have abandoned us

– the long night

I think of you
only fleetingly
just
tinker with you
at the edges
of my thoughts
because
to think of you deeply
and completely
is beyond what
I have the capacity to
withstand

these seconds are
for surviving
but one day
when I am strong
enough
I will let you fill me again
no matter how painful
and unbearable
that will be
as I know that I owe you
that much

— *memorial*

SIGNS OF LIFE

denial
comforts me in the emergency room

anger
overpowers me in the parking lot

hope
tricks me at the train station

depression
stalks me in the bedroom

acceptance
surprises me in the supermarket aisle

— *stages*

LOSS

SIGNS OF LIFE

the white van arrives
on the cusp of dawn
the huff of its engine
intimating your freedom

cocooned on the sofa-bed
I dissociate from the knowledge
that you are clearing our house
of your presence

peeling all the fibres
of memories from the walls
all traces of your musk scent
from the carpet and the sheets

with your army of men
from some cheap company in the southeast
with a thirty percent discount
and price guarantee

your footsteps, hailstones in a storm
foreboding the silence
that will choke me
when the front door clicks shut

when I shall creep
into the barrage of empty space
and deafening vacuity
to start again

– *departure*

do what you want
I don't know how to make you do
what you should

— *defeat*

I won't miss you
you were never here
anyway
I got use to
climbing into a cold bed
while you were
climbing a ladder

all of a sudden
the cold turned to comfort
and your absence
bred ambivalence
until you were just a ghost
sharing my bed
in a space-time
far away from here

— *letting go*

during the night
I sleep
on your side of the bed
your aftershave
still covers the sheets
it's like
you're still here

— *alone*

searching for you
in memories
is like
combing the waves
for sea shells
as they fray at the edges
and crash to shore
under moonlight

it is like
the sting of your sweat
on my lips
and your eyes
washing me clean
with one look
as if to say, I'm sorry
I had to go

— *the search*

I wait for you
on those silent afternoons
as the sun presses
through the curtains
just like those crisp mornings
at the beach
when you strummed my cheek
like a guitar

— *longing*

on the day you left
the trees
hummed in silence
and the sun
frowned
I cried your name
hoping the sky
would
respond
with wet relief

on the night you left
the ocean
licked
your footprints clean
from the sand
and I thought of you
as your sandcastles
faded
from shore
like lost ghosts

— *tears*

I thought
clearing out your clothes
would be cathartic
comforting, perhaps

yesterday I found
the coat you wore
to your last birthday party
in the spring

I remember trying in vain
to make you laugh
in denial of the hollowness
staring back at me

you left me the next day
and I'm not sure
how much clearing out it will take
to forgive you

– abandon

sometimes you are clearer to me
when you are gone
I imagine you like you were
when we met

— *daydream*

forgive me for my coldness
it was never meant for you
though it led you into her arms
and for that
I have betrayed myself

I alone can see
she is just a mirage
seething
on the horizon

while you crawl
towards her in awe
I see the truth looming

like a magic trick that reveals itself
in the end
it is just deceit
and in this game of love
my silence
is the only card I have
left to play

— *replaceable*

SIGNS OF LIFE

two boats
drifting apart on the gulping sea
your shadow growing
ever distant

promises fall away
to the depths below
silently keeping
'til death do us part

and so it seems death
was an easier promise to make
than crossing
this wild ocean with you

— *separation*

on the long road home
there are
no more songs

no more skies
to chase in the shadow
of dusk

I can speak
no more truth
and live
no more dreams

for they are
a language
bereft of you

– the long road

LOVE

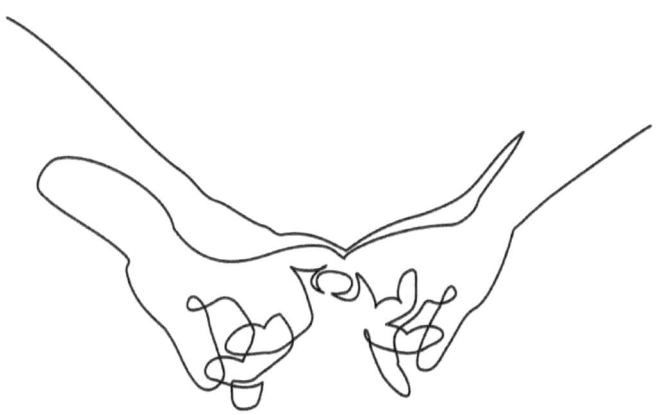

why do we play
these games

is it because we are full
of hate for each other

or because our love is so deep
and aggrieved
that we cannot help
but to hold on

why do you search
for the harshest words when
you wish only to cradle me
skin to skin

and forget the wounds
we have carved into each other

how did we lose ourselves
in a storm so much bigger
than the spark
which gave it birth

and why can I not
find the strength
to break away

— *games*

you used to say
'I love you, but…'
now I know
what 'but' means

– *clarity*

you're my very own
black hole
pulling me in
warping time
killing stars
stealing light

even after
I can no longer stand
I am
weak enough
to come back for more

shower me
with your love
pain
white knuckled passion
that breaks the skin
deeper than any self-love
can reach

and I – a willing ship
steering a course for you
thinking
I can change the tide
if I can only find
your core, where beauty
must lie
beneath the darkness

– *killing stars*

may I suggest
you learn to love yourself
before you expect to find
solace
in another

— *advice*

what kind of love
is the one that makes you
numb
the one that rushes up inside you
and fills you
but hurts
at the same time
what kind of love, is that?

— *kind of love*

fate was cruel
it gave us just
a taste of each other
so strong
so deep
so delicate
were those moments
they vanish
like snowflakes on skin
and my only hope
is to love you in my dreams
like visions
of a life
we may yet share

– ghost

it didn't come quickly
but crept in
silently
and spread like a warm blanket
over my life

I still cannot place the feeling
because the closer I come
to embodying it
the faster it slips away

and yet
I hear it whisper in the night
through your breath
and see it seep through the
curtains at dawn

but never hold it in my palms
to give it shape
or injustice

like a chameleon
changing colours
I glimpse it only
in movement
for were it to stand still
it would overcome me
breathless

— *love elusive*

finding you
was easy
once I stopped looking

—*you*

I miss your beard
the most
and the way it tickles me
when we kiss

— *thoughts of you*

is our love only validated
by a piece of paper
and a cake
or by the number of times
we have held each other together
and cradled each other to sleep
as our worlds
crumbled

– validation

SIGNS OF LIFE

I tried to think of
another word for
love
and yet there was none as
soft
strong
fierce
none that could steal away
my breath
quite as quickly, nor
flood me with tears quite
as painfully
and yet
I wish for no other word
to whisper
to gasp
to cry
in your arms

– a word

I once heard
there are three kinds of love
I think
we have them all

— *three loves*

you always call
so late
my eyelids fail me
but my mind
does not falter
waiting
until the phone rings
to hear your voice
say goodnight

– *long distance*

thankyou
for not wanting me
to lose myself
in you

— *whole*

LEARNING

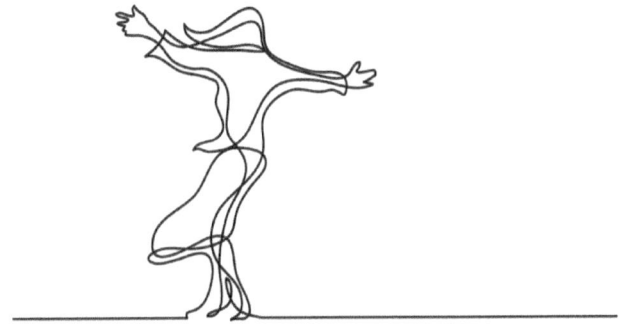

I'm not sure
how to be a woman
unmarried
and childless
my happiness is mistaken
for immaturity
and I bathe in endless questions,
craving for a time of
immaterial fertility

I'm not sure
how to be a mother
unbounding love
and grief
sing to each other across the hall
regrets pass unspoken
as I laugh, and ponder
how much easier it was
to be alone

I'm not sure
how to be a daughter
resentment
and guilt
meld into each other
and I am obscured
by their shadow
when do I get
to be a woman?

– to be a woman

I loathe the feeling of
being overcome
with passion

passion is standing on the brink
ready to lose it all
trusting the fall
and the catcher

but I am neither as brave
nor as naïve as that

– guarded

forgiveness is
the last thing
I have the desire to give
yet I will give it

not because you deserve it
but because I do

—*forgiveness*

I read a book
about resentment
it said
resentment
is worse than guilt

guilt means
you have put yourself first

but resentment is a form
of self-hatred
that will eat you up slowly
from the inside

— *resentment*

all I want
is to see you happy
but you need to step out
of my shadow

— *comparisons*

sometimes the love I have for you
feels like that of a mother

no matter what
I could never desert you

I'm not sure
how to deal with that

— *sister*

drifting with the current is fun
it leads you
to waterfalls

– waterfalls

regret
is my biggest fear

not
that I will say the wrong words
do the wrong things
or hurt the ones I love

but that I will regret it

– fear

SIGNS OF LIFE

the stare
the wink
the dog whistle
the look-up-and-down
the long hug
the brush past
the standing too close
the pressing against
the hand-on-back
the hand-on-arse
the hand-up-skirt
the cheek grab
the breast grope
the *don't be so sensitive.*

— *everyday woman*

here comes the counter-revolution
thumping
like a wave of concrete

do not be troubled
by its menace
do not be fearful
of its anger

it is but a hump in the road
on the way to freedom
which will make the end
that much sweeter

— *staying strong*

SIGNS OF LIFE

I thought these days
I could have it all
why is it
so hard?

— *expectations*

where does the life fall
from the trees in Autumn?
red
orange
yellow
flakes
float lifelessly down, but
nowhere do I see
life itself
in their absence

— *epoche*

my therapist asks
what's the worst thing
that could happen?
it's her way of saying
life will go on

yes
life will go on
but it will be without you
and that's
what I'm really afraid of

— *the worst thing*

most people say
it is hard to stay intimate
as the years go by
why then
do we only grow closer

— *ten years*

life gets you in those moments
when you thought
you could not
endure more
or suffer more
it shows you not what you are capable of
but how far you can break
more than what you thought
your body
and soul
could ever handle
and to come out the other side
shattered
but alive

— survivor

you are so lucky
you have the power
to be sorry

— *apologize*

HOPE

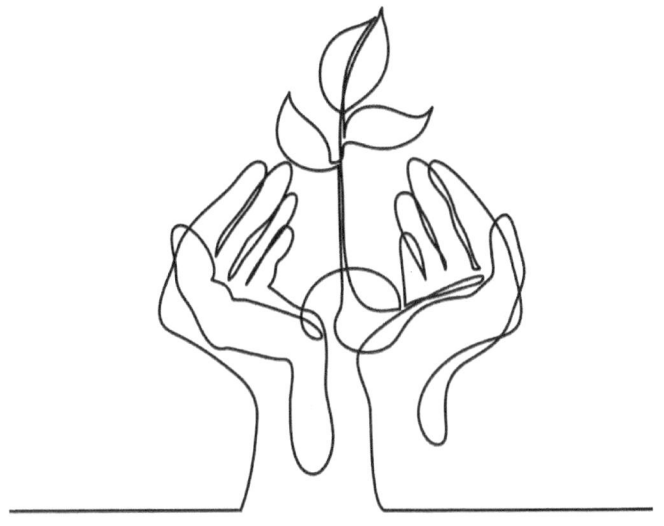

my grandmother has strong hands
they sowed the seeds
of a migrant family
stitch by stitch

late nights working at the factory
for her children
to live a life free of sacrifice

and for her grandchildren
to write poetry
in a language not of her own

for love, above all
and it's warm smell
of clove and garlic and hot charcoal
is the legacy
of courage
of language and culture
not lost, but
reborn in these very words

– *yiayia*

thank you
for all your imperfections
for all the things you fucked up
and put back together again
so I could learn
that you are only human
like me
the only kind of superhero I need

— *imperfections*

we are like lamp posts
appearing
in each other's lives
at milestone moments
tracing our paths
through the darkness
connected only by
the sentimental commitment
of the past

– the path

it is not the sound of thunder
that scares me
but
the moment of silence
just before
when the earth gasps fearfully
in anticipation

                                          thunder sweeps across the field
                                              like a gravitational wave
                                             rolling through the pasture
                                               sucking up the air and
                                                           bang
                                                  a clap in my chest
                                                    resuscitates me

SIGNS OF LIFE

it sounds like a balloon
deflating
when the storm passes over
and floats off
to water someone else's garden

— *three poems for the rain*

the flowers reach upwards
in thirst
begging the sky
for validation

after the rain
they are bruised but fulfilled

— *resilience*

my favourite memories
are of us
playing doctors and nurses
with our teddy bears
maybe our children
will do the same

– *generations*

the best day
is the one before you arrive

I fill the fridge

now I can cook
for two

— *return*

when you trace
the life inside me
and play my belly
like a drum
to teach him rhythm
and soul
before life distracts him
with candy
and smartphones, then
he will remember
deep within
the call of his father
and be guided back
to the tempo
and passion of his birth

– *origin story*

sometimes I wonder
how you will change me
shape me
into someone
I do not recognize

I have built a life
as autonomous as possible
that I am scared to let
dependency
in

what will I become
when you enter my life
and for the first time
I feel reborn?

– to my unborn daughter

this is the house
where lovers danced
and spun romance
within the walls

this is the place
where dreams were made
and children played
along the halls

this is the room
where grief was shared
and partners cared
for ailing love

this is the home
where pain amends
and life ascends
the sky above

— *our house*

touch is
both forbidden
and craved

warm
in its infancy but
subdued with time

a story-teller
in times
of speechless acrimony
carrying the silence
with dutiful strength
and grace

there, in the failure of words
and in the ashes
of promised deeds
touch catches us
and keeps us alive

— *touch*

there is comfort
in these empty pages
so many possibilities
await me

— *pages*

ABOUT THE AUTHOR

Meg Bloom lives in Melbourne, Australia.

www.ingramcontent.com/pod-product-compliance
Lightning Source LLC
Chambersburg PA
CBHW032043290426
44110CB00012B/931